D0990738

Do You Love Me?

Making Healthy Dating Decisions

ABDO
Publishing Company

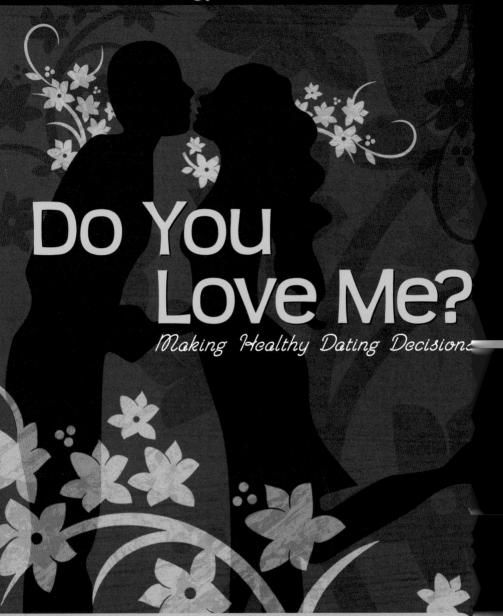

Strong, Beautiful Girls

Do You
Love Me?

Making Healthy Dating Decisions

by Ashley Rae Harris

Content Consultant
Dr. Robyn J. A. Silverman
Child/Teen Development Expert and Success Coach
Powerful Words Character Development

Credits

Published by ABDO Publishing Company, 8000 West 78th Street, Edina, Minnesota 55439. Copyright © 2010 by Abdo Consulting Group, Inc. International copyrights reserved in all countries. No part of this book may be reproduced in any form without written permission from the publisher. The Essential Library™ is a trademark and logo of ABDO Publishing Company.

Printed in the United States.

Editor: Melissa Johnson
Interior Design and Production: Becky Daum
Cover Design: Becky Daum

Library of Congress Cataloging-in-Publication Data
Harris, Ashley Rae.
  Do you love me? : making healthy dating decisions / by Ashley Rae Harris ; content consultant: Dr. Robyn J.A. Silverman.
    p. cm. — (Essential health : strong, beautiful girls)
  Includes index.
  ISBN 978-1-60453-749-9
  1. Teenage girls—Attitudes. 2. Teenage girls—Sexual behavior. 3. Interpersonal relations in adolescence. 4. Teenage girls—Social conditions—21st century. I. Title.

  HQ27.5.H375 2010
  613.9'55—dc22

                                2009002131

Contents

Dr. Robyn Silverman loves to spend time with young people. It's what she does best! As a child and adolescent development specialist Dr. Robyn has devoted her time to helping girls just like you become all they can be. Throughout the Strong, Beautiful Girls series, you'll hear her expert advice as she offers wisdom on boyfriends, school, and everything in between.

An award-winning body image expert and the creator of the Powerful Words Character System, Dr. Robyn likes to look on the bright side of life. She knows how tough it is to be a young woman in today's world, and she's prepared with encouragement to help you embrace your beauty even when your "frenemies" tell you otherwise. Dr. Robyn struggled with her own body image while growing up, so she knows what you're going through.

Dr. Robyn has been told she has a rare talent—to help girls share their wildest dreams and biggest problems. Her compassion makes her a trusted friend to many girls, and she considers it a gift to be able to interact with the young people who she sees as the leaders of tomorrow. She even started a girls' group, the Sassy Sisterhood Girls Circle, to help young women pinpoint how media messages impact their lives and body confidence so they can get

As a speaker and a success coach, her powerful messages have reached thousands of people. Her expert advice has been featured in *Prevention* magazine, *Parents* magazine, and the *Washington Post*. She was even a guest editor for the Dove Self-Esteem Fund: Campaign for Real Beauty. But she has an online presence too, and her writing can be found through her blogs, www.DrRobynsBlog.com and www.BodyImageBlog.com, or through her Web site, www.DrRobynSilverman.com. Dr. Robyn also enjoys spending time with her family in Massachusetts.

Dr. Robyn believes that young people are assets to be developed, not problems to be fixed. She's out to help you become the best you can be. As she puts it, "I'm stepping up to the plate to highlight news stories gone wrong, girls gone right, and programs that help to support strengths instead of weaknesses. I'd be grateful if you'd join me."

Take It from Me

Thinking about dating, making out, or having sex can be scary for adolescent girls. A girl might be unsure of how to talk to boys. She may doubt that she even likes boys, or she might kiss her best friend and wonder if she could be a lesbian. She may struggle with whether to ask someone out. She may even make out or have sex before she is ready. It's important that girls talk to one another and to adults they trust about how to make the right choices during this complicated time.

Starting to become sexually attracted to other people is one of the most exciting things that happens during adolescence. Unfortunately, lots of things that come with the excitement can be scary or painful. No matter who you are and what choices you make, you will probably feel both the thrill and the heartache of sexuality and dating during adolescence. But you can make it easier for yourself by realizing that you are not alone. No matter how weird you feel about something you did, something you thought, or something someone else did, it's a guarantee that many other girls are in the same position.

Part of what makes sexuality so exciting is the mystery behind it. Sexuality is uniquely personal to everyone. As you begin to develop into an adult woman, the changes in your body and your emotional and psychological reactions toward sexuality and dating can be surprising and often challenging. In some situations, you will have to make tough decisions and answer difficult questions. Perhaps the most important questions you will face have to do with what you really want and what feels right to you. Being honest with yourself will help you deal with moments that, let's face it, can be downright awkward.

The key to it all is figuring out how to keep yourself informed and prepared to handle sticky situations, while still enjoying the mystery of a crush or a long-awaited first kiss.

XOXO,
Ashley

1

The Sexy Kids

It seems as though kids look and act older and sexier all the time. The sexing-up of kids affects both boys and girls, but the sexiness of young girls is especially noticeable. Just look at any of your favorite teen stars wearing skimpy clothes, carrying designer handbags, and walking around in five-inch stiletto heels. Even mainstream commercials for hair products and jeans show girls in sexually suggestive positions before they've even reached puberty. It almost seems as though advertisers are trying to shock people by showing girls acting like they are much older and more mature, even though they still look like young kids.

How do these types of images come off to you and your friends, especially when you're very close in age to the girls featured in the sexy ads or television shows? A lot of girls have mixed reactions to sexy kids. On one hand, a girl might look up to other sexy girls who get loads of attention. Some adolescent girls might try on the image of sexiness as they grow older and learn to become more comfortable with their sexuality. Lots of girls follow the lead of their favorite celebs, copying a hairdo or clothing style. It's totally normal to be curious about sexual images and experiment with different styles of clothes and makeup that make you look and feel older—though whether or not your parents will let you leave the house in sexy clothes is another story.

On the other hand, a girl might feel uneasy about acting sexually if she hasn't experienced sex before. It might seem unfair that society focuses on sexiness in girls so much more than boys. A girl might feel that she has less choice about being sexy or not. It might

A lot of girls have mixed reactions to sexy kids.

feel like you have to look sexy in your clothes to look cool. There are tons of different ways a girl might react to the pressure to be sexy. Read on to find out how Margo figured out the difference between sexy and cool.

Margo's Story

Margo was a super-social sixth grader who lived in the suburbs. She had lots of girlfriends and hung out with them constantly. Shopping at the nearest mall was their favorite activity. Even though her mom and dad bought her clothes for school, Margo spent the cash she earned babysitting her younger brother on trendy jewelry, shoes, and clothes. It was important to her that her friends thought her clothes were cool. She stayed away from buying stuff that they seemed to think was "not hot."

Talk About It

- Have you ever found yourself buying something because your friends thought it was cool? How did your purchase make you feel?

- Have you ever tried out a new style? What reaction were you hoping for? How did others react?

One day Margo and her friends were shopping at their favorite store. They liked it because it was cheap and hip. Margo noticed a poster of a girl bent over with a plaid school-uniform-style miniskirt on. Margo could tell that the girl was supposed to seem pretty and hot, but something about the sexual way she was

positioned, and the fact that her pigtails seemed to exaggerate her youth, seemed kind of gross to Margo.

Talk About It

- Have you ever been grossed out by a sexy picture of another girl? What grossed you out about it? Did you tell anyone how you felt? Why or why not?

- How does it make you feel to see kids your own age acting sexy or talking about sex?

Just then, Margo's friend DeDe commented, "That girl is super hot." DeDe's reaction surprised Margo. She almost said something about how she thought the picture was weird but decided against it. A moment later, the two girls were distracted by shrieking from the other side of the store. They laughed and followed the noise.

Margo and DeDe quickly discovered that the shrieking was coming from their other friends, Amy and Maya, who were holding up thong panties. Margo laughed along as her friends made sexy faces and put the thongs on over their jeans.

Talk About It

- Why didn't Margo tell DeDe she thought the picture was weird?

- Do you ever wish that you could look sexier or have sex to be more like the images you see on television and the Internet? Do your friends ever talk about wanting to be sexier?

"I think we should get them," said Amy. "It would be super cute to wear them so they just peeked a little over the top of our jeans."

"Oh totally!" agreed Maya. "The guys would think it was so hot. No boy can resist a thong."

As the other three girls picked out thongs to buy, Margo felt uncomfortable. It didn't make sense to her that they were making fun of thongs one second and then buying them the next. Plus, she didn't know if she liked the idea of showing her underwear, especially at school.

Talk About It

- Have you ever felt uncomfortable with what your friends wanted to do? What was the situation and how did you handle it?

- Why were Margo and her friends making faces and laughing at the underwear?

- Why do you think Margo's friends made fun of the thongs but decided to buy them anyway?

At her friends' urging, Margo ended up buying a purple thong. The girls all agreed to show off their thongs at school the next day. But when Margo got dressed and put on her thong the next morning, it cut into her skin and felt uncomfortable. When she put her jeans on so that the top of the thong was visible,

The girls all agreed to show off their thongs at school the next day.

she felt like she was showing off part of her butt. This made her feel even more uncomfortable because she didn't want to show herself off like that at school. She decided not to wear it.

As soon as she got to school, Margo ran into Amy and Maya. They were both wearing their thongs and immediately tried to look to see if Margo was wearing hers. They rolled their eyes at her when they discovered she wasn't wearing it.

"You're such a prude, Margo," said Maya, as she and Amy laughed. Margo felt like a little baby.

Talk About It

- **Have you ever tried on something that felt too sexy to wear? What did you do?**

- **Have your friends ever teased you or made fun of you? Why did they do it? How did you respond?**

Just then, DeDe walked up to them and Margo noticed she wasn't wearing her thong either.

"You're a prude too!" Amy chided.

"Whatever," DeDe shrugged. "I tried that thing on and it looked ridiculous. There's no way I was going to wear it to school!" It was Amy and Maya's turn to look embarrassed. Margo found herself smiling at DeDe and admiring how she didn't seem to care what

Amy and Maya thought. Margo felt relieved and even a little proud of herself for making the decision to leave the thong at home.

Talk About It

- How do you think Margo and DeDe handled the situation?

- Have you ever been called a prude? How did you feel and what did you do?

- Have you called someone else a prude? Why? How did the person react and how did you feel after you said it?

- What could Margo have done to feel good about her decision even if DeDe hadn't been there?

Being pressured into acting or dressing sexy at a young age can be damaging for an adolescent girl. Instead of focusing on what she likes to do, she can become obsessed with how she looks and whether others approve of her look or find her attractive. It can be devastating for a girl who tries to be sexy, but finds that her peers do not respond the way she had intended.

It's important to recognize that many girls will seek out a sexier image of themselves during adolescence in an effort to determine who they are and who they want to be. It can feel exciting to grow up and notice new feelings that you may never have felt before. Parents can help their daughters grow into these new sexual selves by encouraging safe self-expression and open conversation. All girls develop at their own speed. Bodies and mind-sets change when the time is right for the individual.

Get Healthy

1. The next time you feel uncomfortable about something, ask yourself why. If someone is trying to talk you into dressing or acting in a way that feels wrong to you, try saying no to see how it feels. You may end up making them feel uncomfortable rather than the other way around.

2. Don't tease your friends who are developing earlier or later than you. Even if they don't seem like it, almost all girls feel somewhat self-conscious while their bodies are changing.

3. It's okay to admire someone's style, but look for role models who have other things to offer besides their looks. Don't be afraid to develop your own style and focus on your own talents and interests.

The Last Word from Ashley

Just because something seems sexy or exciting on television doesn't mean it's right for you. We are surrounded by images of sexy girls everywhere, and they are becoming younger all the time. Unfortunately, we live during a time when young girls are regularly targeted online and elsewhere by adult sexual predators. Overly sexualized images of young girls send the message that it is okay to look at or treat girls with the same standards of sexuality as grown women. It is more important now than ever that girls have the space and freedom to develop at their own pace without being forced or trying to force themselves to act older or more mature. So don't stress—whether you feel like you think about sex all the time, or never think about it at all.

2

I Like Your Brother

dolescence is the time when most girls get a lot of crushes. Some girls feel like all of a sudden they notice everyone, and *everyone* is cute: the boy who sits next to you in history class, the kid who skateboards down your block at night, the cashier at the local convenience store, or sometimes even someone totally off-limits, such as a coach. In some cases, a crush is off-limits not because of an inappropriate age gap, but because it could make things awkward in another area of a girl's life. A common crush that falls into this category is a crush on a friend's older sibling.

Most girls experience a crush on a friend's sibling at one point or another while they're growing up. It makes sense that it happens so frequently. Girls spend tons of time hanging out at their friends' houses, and at least one friend is bound to have an attractive sibling. The more time you spend around someone, the more likely you are to develop a crush and the stronger your feelings can become. It's probably because when you

Most girls experience a crush on a friend's sibling at one point or another while they're growing up.

get a chance to know someone better, you like that person for lots of different reasons, not just because he's cute or he's really good at basketball, but because he's cute, good at basketball, funny, smart . . . you get the picture.

Hanging out at a friend's house is a perfect way for a girl to get to know the cute older brother, but that doesn't necessarily make it easy to have a crush on him. If a girl's friend found out, she might get annoyed or worried about losing her friend or her older brother. If a girl's parents found out, they might become worried that something could happen between their daughter and the older brother during a sleepover or other event. Or a girl might just feel silly and uncomfortable around her crush if she feels she is seen as the friend of the little sister instead of a potential girlfriend.

Jill's Story

Jill had a thing for boys who played soccer. She liked how they wore their hair slightly longer than boys who played other sports, and she thought they looked so confident on the field. The fact that Jill loved to play soccer herself only made her more interested in soccer boys. Most of her friends knew that she always got crushes on soccer players and would tease her about one day "marrying her very own David Beckham."

Unfortunately, soccer wasn't too popular in her eighth-grade class. Most boys played baseball or football instead, and the girls were into basketball or softball. But, the soccer team was so small that Jill got a chance to play at every game and became pretty good.

Midway through the school year, a new girl named Mindy started in Jill's class. Mindy had just moved from the East Coast to Ohio, where Jill lived. They had a few classes together and started to become friends.

One day, Mindy asked Jill if she wanted to come over after school to watch television. Jill was excited to see Mindy's house and happy to have a new friend.

Talk About It

- **Do you usually get crushes on people who do a certain activity or look a certain way? Why do you think you tend to fall for similar people?**

- **Have you recently made a new friend? How did you meet? Why do you get along?**

Mindy had mentioned her older brother, Christopher, and complained about how he burped at the dinner table or hogged the computer. Up to this point, Jill hadn't paid much attention when Mindy talked about Christopher—it just sounded like typical sibling rivalry to her—but that was about to change.

As soon as they walked into Mindy's house, Jill heard a boy's voice holler from another room.

"Hey, Mindy, don't even think about going on-line—I'm trying to download an album." A tall, lanky boy of about 15 appeared in front of the two girls. Jill couldn't help but stare at him. He had dimples and slightly curly hair that came just about to his collar and he was wearing cleats. He was quite possibly the cutest boy she had ever seen in real life.

"Who are you?" The boy turned his attention to Jill. She was so nervous she could hardly speak.

"Jill, this is my brother, Christopher," said Mindy. She turned to her brother. "Okay, can you leave us alone now?"

"No problem, just trying to be friendly," said Christopher, cool and relaxed as he walked away smiling.

"Sorry about that," Mindy apologized, rolling her eyes. But there was no need for her to apologize—Jill was in love.

The two girls spent the rest of the afternoon watching television and talking. Jill didn't get a glimpse of Christopher again that day, but she couldn't keep her mind off him.

After that, Jill started getting invited to Mindy's more often. Of course, she was super excited to go, partly because she liked hanging out with Mindy, but also because she hoped to see Christopher.

Jill didn't get a glimpse of Christopher again that day, but she couldn't keep her mind off him.

She purposely tried to dress cuter if she was going over to Mindy's house, and she even changed out of her uniform once when

they came directly from school. This seemed to puzzle Mindy, who said, "You can do whatever you want, but we're just going to hang out and eat nachos."

Talk About It

- Can you think of the cutest person you have ever seen in real life? What made you think that person was so cute? How did you feel being around the person?

- Have you ever felt like you couldn't keep your mind off someone? What was that feeling like?

- Have you ever had a crush on a friend's older sibling? What did you do?

Jill tried to ask Mindy questions about Christopher. She pretended she was only interested because they both played soccer, but she secretly hoped to find out if he had a girlfriend or if he had ever asked about her. For the most part, though, Mindy wasn't too interested in talking about her brother.

Talk About It

- Have you ever liked someone so much that you changed your clothes or wore a certain outfit just because you thought you might see that person? Why did you do that? How did you want that person to react when he or she saw you?

- Have you ever tried to find out information about a crush from another person? Why did you ask someone else instead of talking to your crush directly?

One night when Jill was sleeping over at Mindy's, she heard noises in the kitchen and thought it might be Christopher. She pretended that she was thirsty and wanted a glass of water as an excuse to go down there. Sure enough, he was there, making macaroni and cheese.

"Hey," he said, smiling at her. "Want some?"

"Oh, no thanks," Jill said. She felt so nervous she didn't know what to say.

"Mindy said you play soccer too," Christopher said. Jill couldn't believe her ears. Was he really trying to make conversation with her? Jill was just starting to tell Christopher what position she played when Mindy walked into the room. Mindy shot each of them a weird look that seemed like she was annoyed.

"What are you guys doing? Jill, let's go back upstairs," Mindy demanded. Jill went with her, but she didn't want to. All she really wanted to do was hang out talking to Christopher in the kitchen.

Once the girls were back in her bedroom, Mindy demanded, "What were you guys talking about?"

"Oh nothing, just soccer," Jill replied. She had the feeling she wasn't doing a very good job concealing the excitement in her voice.

"Do you, like, have a crush on my brother or something?" Mindy asked. Jill didn't know what to say. A part of her wanted to tell Mindy the truth, but something about the way Mindy asked made Jill think it might be a bad idea.

"Well, no . . . not really," Jill replied. She could tell from the look on Mindy's face that she didn't believe her.

"He's really an idiot, so if you like him then maybe you're not as smart as I thought you were," Mindy said coldly as she turned out the light.

Jill felt a wave of discomfort wash over her as she lay there in Mindy's dark bedroom. What Mindy said had hurt, but she also felt bad because she thought maybe Mindy was hurt too. After a few moments, she spoke.

Talk About It

- Why does Jill think it is a bad idea to tell Mindy the truth?
- How do you think Mindy would feel if she knew the truth about Jill's crush?
- Have you ever been in a situation where you thought your friend had a crush on your sibling? How did you feel and what did you do?

"Hey Mindy? I guess I did kind of like Christopher," she admitted quietly. The room was quiet for a moment.

"I know, I could tell."

"I didn't know it would bug you so much," Jill told her.

"It's just weird, thinking about my friend liking my brother. I'm sorry I said you weren't smart," Mindy replied.

After the talk, Jill felt better. It was strange, but after telling Mindy the truth, her crush on Christopher faded a little. She still thought he was super cute, but the idea of them ever dating seemed less likely. Eventually, she started getting new crushes on other boys.

Talk About It

- What do you think about the way Jill handled the situation? How do you think Mindy handled it? What would you do differently if you were Jill or Mindy?

- Why do you think Jill's crush on Christopher faded after she told Mindy the truth?

- Have you had a crush that went away? Why do you think your feelings changed?

Having a crush on a friend's older brother can be a difficult experience. On the one hand, a girl has an opportunity to get to know her friend's brother better than most other boys. This can make it easier for her to develop an interest in him that goes deeper than just a regular crush. On the other hand, she may feel like she has to keep her feelings completely to herself. She may be afraid to put her feelings out there because she has more to risk with someone she actually knows. Plus, she may worry that her friend will be uncomfortable with the situation.

Even though Jill had a major crush on Christopher, she was able to recognize that if she tried to pursue him, it could hurt a friend she cares about. She clearly felt that preserving her friendship with Mindy was more important than pursuing a relationship with Christopher. She was able to be honest about how she felt and move on when the time was right.

Get Healthy

1. If you have a huge crush on a friend's older sibling who you feel is off-limits, ask yourself what it is you like about that person. Maybe you can find similar qualities in someone else.

If your friend handles your crush badly, try to put yourself in her shoes. She might be feeling scared that she would lose one or both of you if your crush developed into a relationship.

When you sense that your friend is feeling insecure or uncomfortable, try doing something special for your friend, like getting movie tickets for the two of you, to show her how much the friendship means to you and that you want to spend time with her.

Remember that a crush is just a crush. Your intense emotions may feel overwhelming, but try not to obsess over that one person. Keep up your usual activities and don't neglect your friends.

The Last Word from Ashley

Part of what makes crushes so intense is the feeling of wanting something—or someone—you can't have. A girl can be so obsessed with a crush that she thinks she knows everything about him, but he may turn out to be completely different than her fantasy. It is important that you don't put everything on the line just to pursue someone you have been admiring from afar. Remember, true friendships are much deeper bonds than most crushes could

3

Pregnant Sis

During adolescence, girls often have a lot of uncertainty about dating and sex. A girl may wonder if she should kiss someone she likes, when the right age is to lose her virginity, or how she can make boys like her without coming off as skanky. With all these questions and more, it's no wonder lots of girls look up to older siblings to help them make choices. Watching what an older brother or sister does can help a girl measure her own behavior against what she thinks she's "supposed to do."

Unfortunately, older brothers and sisters are not always ideal role models. Because older siblings are also still growing up and making decisions that will lead them into adulthood, they are likely to make mistakes sometimes too. If a girl has always looked up to them, it can be especially hard for her to watch her older brother or sister make tough decisions. Just as it can be painful when a parent makes a mistake, it is hard to watch an older brother or sister go down the wrong path.

It's even harder for a girl when she is unsure whether her older sibling is doing the right thing. For example, how does a girl know whether her older brother did the wrong thing by having sex with his teenage girlfriend if he says he loves her? One of the especially confusing things that can happen during adolescence is when an older sister gets pregnant as a teenager. One girl might be upset at her older sister's decision to have a baby, but another might look up to a pregnant older sister, or even wish to become pregnant soon

Because older siblings are also still growing up and making decisions that will lead them into adulthood, they are likely to make mistakes sometimes too.

herself. When Desma's older sister got pregnant, she found herself having to decide what she thought about it and how it should affect her own future.

Desma's Story

Desma was a middle child in a family with three brothers and two sisters. Besides her parents and siblings, she lived with her oldest brother's wife and their baby. Needless to say, it was a very full house. With so many people in and out, Desma learned to take care of herself by making her own meals and even buying most of her own clothes. Desma's parents were sometimes too busy with the younger kids to pay much attention to her, but her older sister Carlene watched over her.

Carlene was 16, four years older than Desma. They looked alike, except Desma thought Carlene was far more beautiful than she would ever be. It wasn't just Carlene's beauty that Desma admired—she was also the smartest, funniest person that Desma had ever met. She told jokes that made Desma's stomach hurt from laughing so hard. Desma even liked Carlene's boyfriend, Jacob, because he sometimes let her come along with them on dates to the mall or to the movies. Jacob was a laid-back guy—the kind of guy Desma imagined she might date when she got old enough.

Talk About It

- Do you have an older sibling who you look up to? What are the qualities in her or him that you admire so much?

- Does your older brother or sister have a boyfriend or girlfriend? If so, what do you think about the person or people they date and why?

One day Carlene and Desma were lying on their beds in the room they shared when Carlene announced that she had a secret to share. Desma was excited to hear what it could be.

"I think after we graduate Jacob and I are going to get married," Carlene said, smiling.

"Really? That's so great! Jacob is the best guy," Desma said, excited for her sister, even though she knew graduation was a long way off.

"Thanks. You know, the thing is . . . I'm pregnant, and it would be the best thing for the baby," Carlene said next. Desma was shocked. She couldn't believe what she was hearing. Carlene? Pregnant? She didn't even know that Carlene was having sex, and now she was pregnant!

"I thought you'd be happy for me," Carlene said when she saw Desma's face.

"I am, I guess. It's just . . . well, I always thought you would go to college or something," Desma answered.

"Well, sometimes stuff happens and you just have to go with it," Carlene replied. "I'm going to be the best mom and Jacob will be a great dad."

For the first time in her life, Desma wasn't sure she believed her older sister.

Talk About It

- **How would you feel if you found out your older sister or brother was having sex?**

- **How would you feel if your older sister announced that she was pregnant?**

- **Why might Desma not believe what Carlene is saying?**

In the months that followed, Carlene's belly and Desma's worry both grew. All of a sudden, Desma felt like she had no one to talk to. Before, she had felt so close to Carlene, and they were always laughing. Having each other made their noisy household easier to live in. They used to fantasize about moving into their own apartment and getting cool jobs, but now it seemed like all Carlene wanted to talk about were baby names and plans for her wedding.

Even though Desma hoped everything would work out for her sister, she couldn't help but feel angry with Carlene for getting pregnant. Now, Desma was certain that Carlene wouldn't be able to do all the things she talked about doing before.

But at other times, it seemed as if Carlene was getting special treatment. Now that she was pregnant, it was as if their parents paid more attention to Carlene than ever before. Their mom took Carlene to doctors' appointments and made special soups for her to eat. Jacob even brought her flowers when he found out. Desma felt alone and invisible—and a little bit jealous.

As Carlene got closer to giving birth, Desma felt further away from her. Even though at first he had been sweet and romantic, she noticed that Jacob seemed further away from Carlene too. Sometimes when he came over, he spent the whole time talking to Desma instead of Carlene. Carlene complained when he went out late on the weekends while she was stuck at home with her big belly, and they got into fights.

Even though Desma hoped everything would work out for her sister, she couldn't help but feel angry with Carlene for getting pregnant.

When Carlene finally had the baby, Desma loved her nephew right away. But even though it was supposed to be a joyous occasion, Carlene seemed really depressed. When Desma asked her about it, Carlene just said she felt sad.

Talk About It

- **What would it be like to be pregnant in high school? How would your life change? What would relationships with boyfriends be like?**

- **Why do you think Carlene and Jacob started fighting?**

It didn't help that Jacob only came around twice in the first week to see the baby. Desma started to wonder what would happen if he never married Carlene at all. What would Carlene do with a baby to take care of all by herself? Would she live in their parents' house for the rest of her life? As much as Desma loved and had looked up to her older sister, she realized then that she would do everything in her power to avoid getting pregnant in high school. She wanted the opportunities that Carlene might have lost.

Talk About It

- Have you ever been really close with someone who stopped caring about the things you used to talk about together? How did it feel and how did you react?

- Have you known anyone who's had a baby before they graduated high school?

Ask Dr. Robyn

As painful as it can be to watch an older sibling make a mistake that could change his or her life forever, it can help put things in perspective. Watching Carlene deal with the reality of getting pregnant as a teenager allowed Desma to realize how much hardship lay before her beloved big sister. And it made her think about what she really wanted out of her own life. As difficult as it was to take a good look at the situation, it pushed Desma to decide that she wouldn't fall into the same trap as Carlene. Although Desma looked up to Carlene so much, she was wise enough to see that even someone you love and admire can make a choice that you would not want to repeat.

Get Healthy

1. Make a list of all the things you want to do in your life. They can be anything from "go to medical school" to "learn to play the drums" to "win a string-cheese-eating contest." The point is to think about all the different experiences you would like to have. Then make a list of the different choices you could make that could help or hurt your chances of achieving your goals.

2. Talk to someone you know who got pregnant at a young age. Ask her what it was like to raise a child as a teen and what she

would have done differently if she could redo everything.

3. Remember that there is a time for everything. If you do what you can to make sure you get what you want now, you will have a better chance of experiencing everything you want in life, including continuing your education, having a career, and starting a family one day when you're ready.

The Last Word from Ashley

In many families and communities, it is common for girls to get pregnant before they have completed high school. Some girls may feel pressure to get pregnant at a young age, because they are looking for attention from those around them, they want to keep the baby's father around, or they hope that having a child will mean they will always have someone to love them. Some may not have planned to get pregnant, but never thought it would happen to them. But despite the love they might hope to achieve by getting pregnant, these girls often find that being a young parent is incredibly difficult and might actually prevent them from becoming close to people their own age. Instead of looking for love through getting pregnant, love yourself enough to take advantage of every opportunity that is out there waiting for you.

4

The Skank

een pregnancy is not the only consequence of having sex at an early age. Having sex is a big deal for a lot of reasons. Besides the possibility of getting pregnant, a girl who becomes sexually active while still in school is likely to encounter plenty of other frustrating problems. Although a boy who loses his virginity at a young age may find that other kids look up to him, a girl who becomes sexually active early often finds herself shunned or ridiculed by her peers. Kids may start rumors, call her names like "slut" or "skank," or treat her as though she deserves no respect. Plus, girls who have sex and don't use protection are more likely to contract sexually transmitted diseases (STDs), such as chlamydia, gonorrhea, HIV, genital warts, herpes, or others.

So why would a girl have sex at an early age when so many bad things could happen because of it? Some girls may not be aware of the consequences of having sex too young. Others may be curious to experiment sexually but end up going too far before they are really ready for it. A girl might be trying to get a boy to like her—and thinks having sex could get his attention. Still others might have experienced a sexual act at an even younger age or in a violent situation, such as being molested by an adult. In this case, they may be using sex as a way to express that experience or self-image.

Regardless of why a girl might become sexually active early or be suspected of having sex early, no one

So why would a girl have sex at an early age when so many bad things could happen because of it?

wants to become known as the school skank. Read on to learn what Grace did when she found herself with a bad reputation.

Grace's Story

Ever since Grace was little, sex had been a regular part of her life. Her mom had several different boyfriends and talked about her sex life as if it were no big deal, so Grace didn't think it was a big deal. She sometimes even heard her mom having sex through the thin walls of their small apartment.

Grace's older brother was the same way, bringing girls over and watching pornography on the television in front of her. Grace thought porn was gross and usually yelled at her brother to turn it off, but he just made fun of her.

Talk About It

- **Have you ever heard your parents having sex, or overheard them talk about sex? How did you feel when that happened?**

- **Have you ever seen a porn movie? What was it like and how did it make you feel?**

- **What do you think it's like for Grace when her brother watches porn movies in front of her?**

When Grace turned 13, she started making out with some boys in her neighborhood. It started off with a bunch of kids playing kissing games at night, and it was funny. One girl dared a boy to kiss another girl while everyone watched and laughed. But after a few nights of kissing games, a few of the older boys wanted to take turns going into a dugout at the baseball field with Grace, all by herself. She wasn't sure why they picked her, but she couldn't help but feel a little proud of herself when she saw that the other girls looked disappointed that they hadn't been picked.

Talk About It

- Have you ever played a kissing game? What did you play and how did people act?

- Have you ever been asked to go off privately with just one other person to kiss? Did you go? Why or why not?

- Have you ever been chosen over other girls or had another girl chosen over you? How did either or both of those situations make you feel?

Grace kissed one boy for a while, then the second. She didn't really feel much while she was kissing them—she was just trying not to screw it up, but each of the boys started to get really excited. The second boy got so worked up that he started to put his hands under her shirt and in her pants. It surprised Grace when he did that, and she froze. After it was over, he took off with the other boy she'd just kissed.

After that night, Grace got used to making out with boys in the dugout. It started to become her "thing." If a boy wanted to make out, he would ask Grace, and they would go there. Grace didn't always particularly like the boys she made out with, but she liked being the girl they went to, and she liked how excited they got around her, especially if she let them touch her under her clothes. She could tell she was special because of how jealous it made the other girls.

Talk About It

- How do you think Grace felt when the boy put his hands under her clothes? Why did she freeze? What would you have done if a boy did this to you?

- Why do you think the other girls are jealous of Grace?

- What do other girls do that makes you jealous? Do you think other girls are jealous of you? Why or why not?

The one thing Grace didn't like was people talking about her behind her back. After she started making out with boys in the dugout, it seemed like people were talking about her all the time. Other girls whispered and called her nasty names, like "ho" and "skank." Boys laughed and looked her up and down in the hallway at school. Even some of the teachers looked at her with what seemed like disgust.

The one thing Grace didn't like was people talking about her behind her back.

Talk About It

- Do you know anyone who has a bad reputation? Do you think they really live up to their reputation?

- What is your reputation at school? Are you known as a nerd, or as a jock, or as an artist, for example? Do you deserve your reputation?

- Have you ever talked about another girl behind her back? Why did you do it? How do you think she would feel if she knew what you said?

Grace consoled herself with the fact that boys liked her. She knew she wasn't really a skank. The other girls were just jealous of all the attention she got. After all, all she ever did was kiss the boys and maybe let them touch her a little bit. She didn't want to go any further than that. She knew she was way too young for sex. She hadn't considered it before, but going with those boys had been a dangerous thing to do. If one of them had tried to force her to have sex, she might not have been able to stop him.

But one day when she was standing behind a bookshelf in the library, she overheard two boys talking on the other side. Soon enough, she realized she'd kissed one of them in the dugout earlier that month and that they were talking about her!

"She was completely naked—I saw everything," the boy she kissed was telling the other. "I made her do everything I wanted. Just go up to her and ask. She'll do it with you."

Grace couldn't believe what she was hearing. The boy was lying about what happened. She had never been completely naked with anyone, and she didn't "do" anything besides kiss. She wondered who else was spreading rumors about her. She wanted to set the record straight but realized no one would believe her.

All of the sudden, Grace felt filled with rage. It wasn't fair that people treated her like this when no one ever said anything about the boys. She decided to teach the boys a lesson.

Grace marched around the bookshelf and stood there in front of the two boys. They stared at her, shocked.

Talk About It

- Has anyone ever talked about you behind your back or spread a rumor about you? How did it make you feel?

- Would you confront the boy if you were Grace? Why or why not? If yes, what would you say to him?

"You're a liar," she said to the boy she had kissed. "I never did the things you said. Don't ever plan on trying to make out with me again."

As she walked away, Grace felt proud for standing up for herself. From then on, she decided to stop sharing her body in such an intimate way with so many people. She wanted to wait until she was with someone she truly liked before making out again.

Talk About It

- Have you ever confronted someone for spreading a rumor about you? How did that person react? How did you feel after doing it?

- Can you think of a time when you made a choice to change your behavior? Why did you make that choice?

Girls who have been sexually abused or who grow up in households where sex is treated casually sometimes think casual sex is normal. They may have learned at an early age that being sexual with someone is a good way to show closeness or to get attention.

Grace learned an important lesson. Sharing her body with the boys at school did not mean she had earned their respect or liking. In fact, she probably lost their respect. But instead of going back to her old habit of using her body to get people to like her, she showed that her respect for herself was more important by confronting the loudmouths in the library.

Get Healthy

1. Ask yourself if you are ready to deal with the possible consequences of being sexually active, such as pregnancy, contracting an STD, or getting a "bad reputation." It's absolutely crucial that you put a lot of thought into whether you are ready to have sex or engage in any sexual activity so that you decide in advance what you will or won't do. Prepare yourself in advance and have an exit plan.

2. Though using condoms properly protects against pregnancy and most STDs, the only sure way to protect yourself is by not having sex.

3. Ask your doctor or an adult how STDs are transmitted and whether you need to have an STD test. Check on the Internet, at the health center in your school, or at the back of this book for places to go for free STD and pregnancy testing. These places will also have information about protecting yourself.

4. The next time you watch a television show or movie that portrays teen or pre-teen sexuality, ask yourself if the situations seem realistic to your own experience.

The Last Word from Ashley

Many kids who have sex at a young age develop a reputation—the difference is that boys are usually seen as studs but girls are usually seen as skanky. It's an unfair double standard, but being aware of it in advance might help a girl avoid making choices that she may regret later. Remember that you're the only person who has any rights to your body—be proud of it and keep it safe.

5

Not Ready

sing your body to get attention often makes you popular for all the wrong reasons. But how does it feel to be a girl who never makes out with boys or dates at all? What about the girl who has no clue what to say to a boy she likes, or isn't even sure she's interested in dating? Just as it can be lonely and embarrassing to be known as the skank, it's not a whole lot of fun to be known as the prude either. Girls who have nothing happening in their dating lives might feel ashamed or feel like they are missing out on something.

Even though there are probably more kids in junior high who are not making out or going on dates than those who are, a girl might feel like she's the only one without experience. Remember Margo, who didn't want to wear a thong that would show her butt to the whole school? There is so much pressure on kids today to be sexual and "in the know" about dating that a girl might actually feel like something is wrong with her if she hasn't kissed someone. She might be worried that no one thinks she's cute enough to ask out. Or she might feel ashamed if she simply isn't ready yet.

In reality, lots of kids feel uncomfortable about getting physical with another person during adolescence. After all, it's a big deal to share your body with someone else, even if all you're doing is holding hands. Many girls are self-conscious about changes in their bodies and might want to keep these new developments to themselves. Whatever the reason, it's totally normal, and in most cases a good idea, to wait until you're really ready to start dating and making out. But that doesn't mean it's always easy.

> **In reality, there are lots of kids who feel uncomfortable about getting physical with another person during adolescence.**

Nicole's Story

Ever since she was a little girl, Nicole wanted to be a famous dancer. She practiced every day after school and even performed at theaters downtown. The kids at school sometimes treated her like a celebrity, especially during the times when she was performing and was

allowed to leave school early to dance. The only bad thing about dancing was that sometimes she spent so much time doing it she felt like she didn't get to hang out with other kids who weren't dancers.

On the first day of her seventh-grade year, Nicole noticed that none of the other girls tried to talk to her about her summer or ask her about dancing. Instead, they all seemed to be trying to get Heather's attention. Nicole noticed that Heather looked totally different than she had last spring. It was like her boobs had grown from nothing to a C-cup overnight, her hair was cut in stylish layers, and she had on tight jeans like the ones Nicole's mother wouldn't let her buy. Nicole could see why the other girls wanted to hang around her, but it wasn't until fifth period that Nicole found out the real reason why Heather was suddenly Miss Popularity.

It turned out that Heather had hooked up with the hottest guy in eighth grade, Will Jones, over the summer. Now all the girls were trying to become her new best friend in the hope that they would get a chance to go out with one of his friends.

Talk About It

- Can you think of a "Miss Popularity" at your school who all the girls seem to want as their friend? Why do you think she is so well liked?

- Do you know anyone who came back to school with dramatic physical changes? How did those changes make that person's life different?

Nicole had never hooked up with any guys. She'd never even talked to a guy on the phone. She was always so busy dancing, she didn't think about it much. But all of a sudden it seemed like it was all anyone cared about. Nicole started to hear about girls sneaking out of their houses to make out with guys at night. There were rumors that two kids got caught kissing during gym class.

Nicole was secretly kind of grossed out by the idea of tongue-kissing someone, but she kept that to herself around her friends from school. The girls Nicole hung out with at school seemed obsessed with talking about who they were texting or kissing or trying to date. These conversations made her uneasy, and she felt like she had nothing to say. Now that no one asked her about dancing, Nicole felt invisible. Certainly the boys weren't paying any attention to her, and now none of the other girls were either.

Talk About It

- Do your friends talk about dating and guys a lot? Have you ever felt out of place during those conversations? Why or why not?

- Have you ever kissed a guy? If yes, why did you do it and how was it the same or different than you expected it to be?

- Can you think of a time when you felt invisible? Why did you feel that way and what did you do about it?

Feeling out of place with her school friends, Nicole spent even more time at the dance studio. Dancing distracted her from feeling like some sort of freak. Plus, at least at the studio people seemed interested in talking to her about something besides making out.

One day Nicole was in the bathroom when Heather "Miss Popularity" walked in. Nicole pretended not to notice her since they had never really spoken before. Besides, Nicole was sure Heather thought she was a total loser. To her surprise, Heather stopped and said, "Hey."

"Oh, hey," Nicole replied.

"You're a really good dancer, right?" Nicole was surprised that Heather seemed to be making friendly conversation with her.

"Um, yeah, I guess," Nicole mumbled shyly.

"That's really cool. I wish I knew how to dance like that," Heather replied, and smiled before entering the stall.

Nicole was surprised that Heather seemed to be making friendly conversation with her.

Nicole couldn't believe it. The coolest girl in school, the one who all the boys were after, had just told Nicole that she wished she could be more like her! After months of feeling like she was lame for not wanting to make out, Nicole actually felt good about herself. And she couldn't wait to get to dance practice after school.

Talk About It

- Do you have a passion similar to Nicole's? What is it, and why does it make you happy?

- Have you ever been surprised that someone you admired thought you were cool, or admired something about you too? What was that like?

Nicole's brief conversation with Heather taught her an important lesson. No matter how beautiful, popular, or perfect someone might seem, there are always qualities that she notices in someone else and wishes she had. But if a girl makes the right choices and stays true to herself instead of pretending to be something she's not, she will accomplish things that make her feel proud.

A lot of girls feel ashamed or self-conscious because they're not more experienced with boys and dating. You may not realize that most of your friends are probably feeling awkward too! It's perfectly normal for an adolescent girl to be hesitant about sharing her body in an intimate way. Unfortunately, girls are made to feel like something is wrong with them if they're not ready to be sexual when their classmates or friends are.

Get Healthy

1. If you notice that you and your friends are talking about boys all the time, try to change the subject every once in a while. It's fine to be interested in dating, but don't act so boy-crazy that you forget about all the other things you love to do and talk about.

2. Don't make out with someone just to "get experience." If you are really feeling out of the loop and have questions, ask an adult you trust or an older sibling about what to expect. This may help you decide when the time is right for you and prepare yourself for it.

3. Avoid calling other girls mean names, such as skank or prude. Recognize that dating and sexuality are complicated and everyone needs to figure out how to deal with it on their own. Other people's decisions about sexuality are theirs alone to make—even if you don't agree with their decisions—and nobody likes to be judged.

The Last Word from Ashley

It's important to keep in mind that everyone is ready to date and be physical with other people at different times. It's not like there's a magic age when suddenly everyone is ready to start making out and something is wrong with you if you don't participate. Being confident about yourself and your interests draws and attracts others to you, whether or not you date or make out with them. In fact, people are more likely to trust your judgment and value your opinions if you always go with your gut instead of forcing yourself into something that isn't right for you.

6

Trying
It Out

There are plenty of girls out there who are more interested in having a girlfriend than a boyfriend. But kissing another girl doesn't necessarily mean a girl is a lesbian or bisexual. Maybe she was just curious to know what it felt like to kiss someone. A lot of girls trust their close female friends with their secrets or insecurities much more than they do their male classmates, and feel less embarrassed around them when doing something new or uncomfortable. It is not uncommon for girls to try out kissing or other sexual activity for the first time with other girls.

Sometimes girls kiss other girls for different reasons—not because they are attracted to them, or because they are experimenting with sexual activity for the first time. With the increased pressure to look and dress sexier, there is an expectation that girls also behave sexier at an earlier age. In an effort to live up to the expectation of being sexual, some girls purposely act extra sexy in public. Some girls even try to prove how sexually mature they are to other kids by making out with their girlfriends at parties or even at school.

In an effort to live up to the expectation of being sexual, some girls purposely act extra sexy in public.

Trying to figure out who you are as a sexual person isn't easy, especially when most of the sexual feelings you have are totally new to you. It is common for girls to feel a lot of different emotions about sex at the same time. So if you've kissed a girl, how do you know which category you fall into? Are you a lesbian? Were you just curious? Were you hoping to get attention from other kids?

Liv's Story

Liv knew she was part of the in crowd at school. Her parents gave her plenty of money to buy all the newest and hippest clothes. She had a later curfew than most of her classmates and was allowed to go on boy-girl group dates when she was 13. She was also allowed to spend a lot of time with boys outside of school. Because of that, she didn't feel as intimidated by boys her own age as some of the other girls she knew were. She actually felt the opposite; it seemed like boys were more nervous around her and her friends.

Liv's best friend, Kelly, was almost like her twin. They spent all their time together, dressed alike, and even had the same hairstyle and giggle. The two girls usually sat with a big group of boys during lunch. Most of the time everyone talked about new, juicy photos on their friends' blogs or made fun of the gross food in the cafeteria. Sometimes the boys acted silly and asked Liv and Kelly dirty questions, like if they'd ever touched a boy's privates, but the girls just laughed and made fun of them for "acting like perverts." Neither girl took the boys' questions seriously and both considered these boys to be their friends.

Talk About It

- **Do you feel comfortable with boys your own age or do you feel intimidated by them? Have boys ever acted nervous around you and your friends in social situations?**

- **Are there many girl-boy groups of friends that hang out together at your school, or do they stay separate? Why do you think that is?**

- **Has a boy ever asked you personal sexual questions? Did you tell him the truth? Why or why not?**

One Friday night, Liv and Kelly were going to a movie with two guy friends, Troy and Derek. Derek's older brother, Kevin, was supposed to drop them off on his way to a party. Liv had a secret crush on Kevin, who was a sophomore in high school. Only Kelly knew about it. Since they knew Kevin would be driving, the girls decided to dress up extra sexy. Kelly wore a super short skirt with tall boots and Liv wore a shirt that showed her midriff with tight jeans. They both agreed that they looked hot and hoped Kevin would notice.

Liv could tell right away that Kevin noticed how they looked. He kept glancing in the rearview mirror at them while they talked and laughed with Derek and Troy in the backseat. This made Liv feel bold, and she decided to flirt with Kevin a little bit.

"How's it going, Kevin?" she asked, giggling. Kelly started giggling too.

"Yeah, how's high school life?" laughed Kelly. Kevin shook his head but smiled at their teasing tone.

After awhile, Kevin started teasing them back a little.

Talk About It

- Do you and your friends ever try to dress up sexy for boys? What kind of reaction do you get and how does it make you feel?

- Is it easier to dress or feel hot when you are with another friend than it is when you are on your own? Why?

- Have you and a friend ever flirted with a boy at the same time? If so, why? How did the boy react?

"You girls look pretty dressed up tonight. Are you sure you want to sit in a movie theater? Maybe we should do something else," he suggested.

"Like what?" Liv asked. She looked over at Derek and Troy but couldn't tell what they were thinking from their expressions.

"We could go to the park," Kevin said.

Liv and Kelly made eye contact with each other and shrugged—why not? They both were thrilled to get a chance to hang out with Kevin.

When they got to the park, they sat around talking. Eventually the conversation turned to sex. Kevin asked Liv and Kelly if they'd ever kissed a boy or taken off their shirts in front of anyone. The girls acted really casual and pretended like they had more experience than they really did.

When they got to the park, they sat around talking. Eventually the conversation turned to sex.

"So what kind of stuff did you do?" Kevin pushed further. Liv was trying to think about what would impress him, when suddenly it just popped out.

"We've made out with each other," she said confidently. She didn't look at Kelly.

"Really? Well why don't you do it right now then?"

Liv hesitated, but then said, "It's not a big deal." She glanced at Kelly, who seemed nervous.

Then all of a sudden, Kelly said, "Fine," and grabbed Liv and started to kiss her.

It only lasted for a couple of seconds, but the boys laughed and made whooping and hollering sounds.

Talk About It

- **Have you ever pretended that you had more experience than you actually did? Why?**
- **Have you ever kissed another girl? If so, how did it happen and what was it like?**

Liv couldn't believe she'd just kissed a girl. She felt proud of the way the boys reacted. Even Kevin seemed impressed.

After they got dropped off, the two girls gossiped about the way the boys had reacted. Both felt the thrill of having done something naughty and gotten away with it. And they both agreed that since they didn't really like it, they definitely weren't lesbians.

As fun and harmless as the kiss seemed that night, Liv and Kelly were not prepared for the way people reacted when they returned to school on Monday. It was like everyone knew and was talking about it. Other girls whispered and stared at them. At lunch the boys couldn't stop bugging them about it and trying to get them to do it again. At first Liv just laughed, but something about the whole situation didn't feel right.

She was a little upset that the boys had told other people about the kiss. Liz was starting to wish she hadn't talked about sex with them. She worried about what other secrets they might have told. She felt like she couldn't trust Troy, Derek, or Kevin anymore.

Talk About It

- Have you ever told a secret you wish you hadn't? Why did you tell it? How did you feel afterward?

- Has a friend ever betrayed your trust? What happened? What did you do about it?

Meanwhile, Kelly seemed to be enjoying the attention. At one point, she even put her arm around Liv's shoulder, which made Liv so uncomfortable that she excused herself to use the bathroom.

Once in the stall, she saw that someone had scrawled "Liv the Lesbo" on the wall. She wanted to cry. She had only wanted Kevin to think she was cool and sexy, but she'd never intended to keep kissing Kelly or act like she wanted to. At lunch the boys had treated Kelly and Liv like a spectacle, not like friends. Liv was worried they would never see her in the same way again. But mostly, she was worried that her friendship with Kelly would change because of the kiss.

Talk About It

- Have you ever done something to get attention that you later regretted? What did you do and what made you regret it?

- How can Liz make things feel more normal and comfortable with her friends again? What would you do if you were in her situation?

Even though Liv originally wanted to get a reaction from the boys by kissing Kelly, she ended up feeling really uncomfortable with the kind of attention the kiss invited. Plus, it created an awkward situation between her and Kelly since Kelly wanted to continue playing the role even though Liv did not.

Sometimes girls feel like they have to act in an obviously sexy way to get boys or other kids to notice them, and it ends up backfiring. They might have the misconception that other kids are experienced when in reality most are just as new to sexuality and not entirely comfortable with it yet either. Rather than trying to do what you think others want you to do, it's important for you to trust and listen to yourself when it comes to your sexual choices. What does the voice inside your head say? What is your gut trying to tell you? Girls who take ownership of their own likes or dislikes at an early age are more likely to develop healthy relationships and enjoy themselves when they are finally ready to engage in sexual activity.

Get Healthy

1. Next time you're having a sex talk with a group of friends, consider answering their questions honestly. You might be surprised to find that most other kids (including boys)

are less experienced than they might have originally let on.

2. Refuse to answer a question that feels too personal to you. Ask yourself why you felt like you had to answer it in the first place. Observe how other kids react when you create a boundary of okay versus not okay conversation topics.

3. If you find yourself regretting a sexual choice that you made, make a list of the positive and negative things that happened because of it. Then write down how you can make a better choice next time.

The Last Word from Ashley

Girls kissing other girls can be a fantasy in our culture, and adolescent girls sometimes use it to get attention or show their peers that they are sexual. Unfortunately, it can create some unexpected problems for adolescent girls who have to face the gossip at school. Even though people might pressure a girl to kiss her female friend, they are just as likely to turn on her and make her feel like a freak if she actually does it. Plus, using a close friendship to act out sexually in public can put strain or distance between you and your friend. The important thing is to make choices, especially sexual ones, based on what you really feel and want instead of using

7

Coming Out

*L*iv made out with her best friend Kelly to get attention from an older boy they both wanted to impress. She certainly got the attention she was looking for—and then some. But there are plenty of girls who would rather not receive any attention at all for making out with other girls. In fact, they might want to kiss another girl, but decide not to because they are so worried about what other people might think. Whereas Liv and Kelly tried to show off by kissing each other because they were really interested in the boys who were around, a girl who is actually interested in other girls might feel ashamed of her feelings and worried that someone will find out.

Today, a lot of kids are much more accepting of being gay than in earlier years. It is becoming normal in many middle and high schools for a girl to walk down the hallway holding hands with her girlfriend or for a boy to take another boy as a date to the school dance. Increasing numbers of teachers and parents teach kids sexual tolerance along with antiracism or antisexism.

But there are still plenty of people and communities that believe attraction between same-sex people is wrong or sinful. A gay person might be treated as a freak or even a danger to his or her classmates. The preteen and teen years can feel awfully lonely for someone who is not accepted by the other people at school or in the community. It is important for teens in this situation to find at least one person they trust who they can talk to about these issues.

The preteen and teen years can feel awfully lonely for someone who is not accepted by the other people at school or in the community.

Missy's Story

Missy lived in a small town about 30 miles outside of the city. She had two older brothers and they all spent a lot of time helping their parents in the family shop. In exchange for helping, the three kids were allowed to take their dad's car into the city once a week to eat, see movies, shop, and hang out. Sometimes Missy brought her best friend Tara along with them on the trips to the city.

Missy and Tara had been friends for five years, since they were nine. They met when Tara first moved to town. Missy liked Tara right away because she knew fun games and had the best taste in movies. Plus, Tara was from the city and had tons of stories about her old school, which had hundreds of kids from all over the world. It sounded so cool and different to Missy, who had always gone to school with the same 50 kids.

Tara told Missy about one of her friends, Sasha. Sasha was an average girl in every way—except she had two moms. Where Tara came from, some kids had two moms or two dads and it wasn't a big deal. Gay parents showed up to school events, and there were even teachers who were gay. Everyone knew about it and no one seemed to really care. Missy couldn't imagine that.

When most of the people Missy knew talked about gay people, they usually acted like they hated them or were afraid of them. Some people called them freaks or sinners.

Talk About It

- Do you know any people who are gay? What do other people say about them and how are they treated?

- Do you or any of your friends have gay parents? What do you think it would be like to have a parent who was gay? How might it be the same or different as having a parent who is straight?

Missy was interested in the people in Tara's stories because they sounded so different from the people she knew. But she also was interested for another reason—she thought sometimes that she herself might be gay. She had never had a crush on a boy, but she regularly thought about kissing other girls. She noticed the girls who were pretty and wished she could touch their hair. Whenever she had these thoughts, she felt super embarrassed and tried to think about something else. She worried that someone might be able to tell what she was thinking about. And she felt like something was wrong with her. All the other girls at school seemed to be obsessed with which boy was the cutest.

Missy would play along, pretending to agree while they talked, but the whole time she would wonder inside why she didn't feel the same way.

Talk About It

- **Have you ever felt the urge to kiss or touch another girl? How did you feel about yourself when you had those thoughts?**

- **Have you ever pretended to feel something you didn't so you would fit in at school? How did pretending make you feel?**

One Saturday Missy and Tara drove into the city with Missy's brothers and asked to be dropped off at a clothing store they'd read about online that sold cool dresses and boots. When they walked in, they saw that the place was really small and was filled with weird stuff.

"Look at this!" Missy said, holding up a pair of pants lined in fur.

"You could totally pull those off," Tara said and they laughed.

Just then a girl picked up the pants and looked at them. Then she looked straight at Missy and smiled.

"I think they'd look great on you," she said. Missy felt a rush go through her that she'd never felt before. She felt herself blush deeply. The girl noticed and smiled again before walking away. Then Missy watched the girl put her arm around another girl's waist. She couldn't believe what had just happened.

Missy felt a rush go through her that she'd never felt before.

"Hello? Hello? Are you there?" Tara's voice snapped Missy back to reality.

"Oh, yeah . . ." Missy mumbled.

"That girl was kind of weird," Tara frowned as she looked at Missy's face. "I think she wanted you or something."

"What? No way," Missy tried to play it cool. She quickly added, "That's gross."

"Whatever," Tara shrugged, turning back to the clothes.

Talk About It

- **Why do you think Tara thought the girl was weird?**

- **Why did Missy tell Tara she thought it was gross to think about a girl wanting her?**

After that day, Missy thought about the girl in the store all the time. She wished desperately that she could see her again or talk to her. It was even harder

because she couldn't tell her friends or family about her feelings. She knew her family wouldn't understand.

Missy started to visit Web sites for girls who liked other girls. She read message boards with different topics for teenagers and learned that some of the girls were a lot like her and some were totally different. In some ways, chatting online made Missy feel better. She could tell her frustrations to people who had been through it themselves. However, she used a screen name and knew better than to give out personal information. But getting sympathy online just wasn't a real substitute for talking to someone in person.

She worried more and more about the secret she was keeping. She felt like she couldn't tell anyone. It got to the point that she felt awkward hanging out with people at school. She still hung out with Tara, but it seemed like they had less to talk about. She was afraid that if anyone at school found out she was gay, they would tease her or stop talking to her. Nobody at her school had ever come out of the closet, and Missy was terribly afraid to be the first.

Talk About It

- Have you ever gotten involved in an online community? What did you like or dislike about it?

- Why do you think Missy feels like she and Tara have less to talk about?

Eventually Missy started going into the city without Tara. While her brothers were doing their own thing, Missy would go to coffee shops and meet other girls, and they would talk and walk around. Sometimes the girls acted like they wanted to kiss her, but she felt so nervous that she always came up with an excuse to go home.

Then one day at a coffee shop, Missy saw the girl from the clothing store. She couldn't believe it.

She couldn't help staring; the girl was so beautiful. Then the girl noticed her and smiled the same way she'd smiled the day in the shop. Eventually she walked over and introduced herself.

"I'm Jia. I met you at that store, right?"

"Yeah," Missy found herself blushing again. "I'm Missy."

They ended up hanging out, talking for the next hour until Missy's brothers came to pick her up. Then Jia asked her if she could call her. Missy had never felt so happy in her entire life. Jia started calling a lot and they would talk for hours on the phone.

Most of the time, Missy's heart felt like it would leap out of her chest, but she also felt anxious.

She wished she could tell someone about Jia. It was like she was living a double life that made her feel lonely when she was with her family or hanging out with Tara.

Talk About It

- **Have you ever liked someone? Did he or she like you back? How did it make you feel?**

- **Have you ever had a secret you felt you couldn't share with anyone? How did that feel?**

Finally, one day Missy decided to take a big risk and tell Tara about Jia. She was sick of keeping everything to herself. She was afraid but hoped Tara would understand.

"I have to tell you something," Missy began slowly. "I'm kind of seeing someone."

"Really?! Oh my gosh, who?!" Tara bubbled, thrilled for her friend. Missy almost chickened out when she saw how excited Tara was.

"Well . . . do you remember that girl from the clothing store?" Missy finally stammered. There was a silence and Missy shut her eyes tightly, trying not to cry. "I was so nervous to tell you."

"Hey," Tara said, "that's cool. It's great. I can't wait to meet her."

Missy was so relieved to hear those words come out of Tara's mouth, and to have finally said it. At least now there was one person who knew the truth.

Talk About It

- If you were in Missy's situation, would you tell Tara your secret? Why or why not?

- How would you react if you found out one of your friends was gay?

Being openly gay can be hard in today's society, especially if the people in your life see homosexuality as wrong. Coming to terms with your sexuality is difficult enough in a supportive environment. It's even more difficult if you feel you have nowhere to turn. Missy felt so alone with her secret that the only place she felt comfortable discussing her feelings was on a Web site.

Luckily, Missy learned to feel more comfortable with her sexuality as she met girls who were like her—just regular girls who liked other girls. This helped her find enough courage to tell Tara the truth and take the first step to being more honest about her true feelings with those she cares about. And, she gave Tara a chance to be the supportive friend she'd always been.

Get Healthy

1. If you think that you might be interested in other girls, you are not alone. There are lots of other kids out there who are coming to terms with their homosexuality. Find a support group online for gay teens to read about how other kids in similar situations deal with—and survive—being gay in middle and high school.

2. If you are gay, find someone to talk to about it. Locate one person who you can trust with the truth. It's important not to lose touch with people who care about you. Give them a chance to be supportive!

3. Be sensitive to kids at your school who might be gay. Don't participate in gay-bashing, and don't use the term "gay" as an insult.

4. It's good to find a supportive online community, but be careful IM-ing strangers or talking to them in chat rooms. Never share personal or identifying information online.

The Last Word from Ashley

Nowadays, many kids are used to seeing movie stars, Olympic athletes, musicians, and other celebrities who are gay. There are even pop songs about girls kissing other girls. Still, while many kids are more tolerant of homosexuality than they ever were in the past, it is still pretty normal for a girl to feel awkward and scared if she realizes she's more interested in other girls than boys. The most important thing to realize about sexuality is that it's not so much about whether you like girls or boys—it's about feeling comfortable with yourself. Over time, you will learn to feel more confident about your sexuality in situations with people who are less tolerant. For now, find trustworthy friends and adults who make you feel safe.

8

Can We Hang Out?

There are few things more nerve-racking than asking someone out who you really like. It gets a little easier with practice and experience, but it's always hard to put yourself out there, knowing that you could get rejected. Even the least shy girl still might have a hard time telling a guy that she's interested in him.

If it's so painful, what's the point in doing it? Some girls think they should just wait for boys to come to them. But there are just as many guys as girls who can't work up the nerve to ask a girl out. Plus, many people disagree that it's "the boy's job" to ask the girl out. Instead, some people think it is perfectly acceptable for girls to ask boys out. Why wait for a boy to come around when you can find one for yourself? Still, that doesn't mean he'll always say yes or that it won't be awkward.

Sometimes your friends may push you to "make a move" or offer to ask the guy for you. In some situations this might be helpful. Having a friend do the asking could help you feel less nervous. However, being pushed by your friends before you're ready can create an uncomfortable situation. Read on to find out how to ask a guy out with style, and avoid feeling lame if it doesn't work out.

Why wait for a boy to come around when you can find one for yourself?

Benna's Story

Benna had had a crush on Eric for at least a year. She colored his name in her notebooks at school and had daydreams about calling him her boyfriend. Her friends teased her about it and even taped a picture of Benna next to one of Eric torn out of the yearbook. It was so funny, she kept it inside her locker.

The eighth grade spring dance was coming up and Benna wanted to go with Eric more than anything. Her friends all told her that she should just ask him, but she wasn't sure. Eric didn't seem to notice her at all and they'd never really spoken to each other. Benna thought that she should at least have a conversation with Eric before asking him out. Her friends were beginning to bother her so much that she sometimes wished she'd kept her crush secret.

Talk About It

- **Have you ever asked someone out? Were you nervous before you did it?**

- **Would you ask out a guy who you'd never spoken to? Why or why not?**

- **Have your friends ever pressured you into asking someone out? How did that make you feel?**

One night, Benna and her friends were all sleeping over at her friend Jasmine's house. All the girls were trying to convince her to ask Eric to the dance. "He'll totally go with you," said Jasmine, and everyone agreed. Another friend entered a text into Benna's phone, while Benna hid her face in a pillow.

"'Will you go to the spring dance with me? Benna.' We're pressing send now . . ." warned the other girls, as Benna squealed. She jumped up and tried to grab the phone away at the last minute. Something

about this just felt like a bad idea. If she was going to ask Eric out, she at least wanted to have one conversation with him first.

"Sent!"

All the girls were excited to see what he'd write back, except Benna, who felt like she might actually

Something about this just felt like a bad idea. If she was going to ask Eric out, she at least wanted to have one conversation with him first.

throw up. Finally the reply came: "'Who is Benna?'"

Benna's heart sank, and the mood in the room shifted. Suddenly everyone's excitement seemed to turn to awkwardness. Benna felt humiliated that he

didn't even know who she was—even though everyone else knew how big of a crush she had on him.

Benna tried to laugh off Eric's reply, but she still felt like a loser a few weeks later. She knew she had to do something to save face, but she didn't know what.

One afternoon during debate team after school, Benna was talking to her friend Marco. She and Marco had been friends all year since joining the team.

"So are you going to the spring dance?" Marco said. Benna felt the familiar shame of the night at Jasmine's come over her.

Talk About It

- Have you ever had a crush on someone who didn't know who you were? Did you ever get to know him better? If so, did your crush on him change at all and how?

- What would you do if you were Benna to "save face"?

- Have you ever done something to save face before? What was it and how did it turn out?

"Don't even ask," Benna rolled her eyes. She definitely didn't want to talk about the Eric incident. To her surprise, Marco turned bright red. A light bulb went on in Benna's head. Marco wasn't talking about Eric. Benna realized she had been so embarrassed about her failed attempt to ask Eric out that she hadn't noticed Marco was trying to ask her to the dance.

"Never mind, it's just an embarrassing story," Benna tried to recover. "It's always weird trying to figure out who to go with, you know?"

"Oh, yeah, totally," Marco said, looking slightly relieved.

Benna took a deep breath. "If you don't have a date, maybe we should go together," she said before she lost her nerve.

"That would be awesome!" Marco said, which made Benna smile. She thought to herself that maybe asking a guy out isn't the worst thing in the world, just as long as you do it your own way.

Talk About It

- Have you ever not realized someone liked you until it was too late? What happened?

- Can you think of a situation when you tried something a second time even though the first time you had a bad experience? What happened?

Benna's friends pushed her into asking Eric out before she was ready. She felt comfortable and confident around Marco and made the choice on her own. Deciding to ask someone out should never be anyone else's decision but your own.

The cool thing about asking a guy out is that it sets the stage for a more equal relationship between you and the guy. Once you've shown that you are confident enough to ask him out, it becomes easier to be open and say what you want in other situations. You've made it clear that he doesn't get to call all the shots, like deciding what movie to see or when and whether to have a physical relationship. In the end, a girl's likely to be happier in any situation where she feels comfortable and safe about saying and doing exactly what she wants and thinks. Relationships with guys are no exception. Plus, taking a bold risk like asking someone out can help a girl realize she can survive even the most intimidating situations.

Get Healthy

1. Even if you don't feel confident asking a guy to go out with you, try inviting him to a group hangout. That way, if he says no you won't feel like it's personal. If he says yes, it might give you the confidence to ask him

2. Talk to your dad or an older brother about what it was like to date when they were your age. You might be surprised to know that they, like most boys, were probably just as nervous about asking someone out as you are.

3. When in doubt, think casual. Rather than being super romantic toward a guy you're still trying to get to know, such as pouring your heart out in a sappy card, try e-mailing him a funny video you found online. The less pressure you put on yourself or him, the better your chances of getting to know each other in a fun, lighthearted way.

The Last Word from Ashley

The whole point of asking a guy out is to try to get to know him better, and to take a risk that might be worth it in the end. What's the worst that can happen? He says no and you feel embarrassed for a little while. Sooner or later, you'll move on and it will stop being such a big deal. And there's always a chance he'll say yes . . . after all, maybe he is interested, and hoping that you will make the first move. The important thing to remember is that there is no shame in making what you want clear—just don't let your friends send the text for you.

A Second Look

Throughout this book, we have followed a girl who asked a guy out for the first time, another girl who kissed her friend to get attention, a girl who became known as the school skank, and a girl who discovered that being the only girl not dating might actually have some advantages.

Some of these stories have been intense. At times they may have been a little uncomfortable to read. If you felt uncomfortable at times while reading this book, you may have asked yourself what was making you feel that way. Perhaps it has something to do with the fact that when it comes to sexuality, we don't always have a clear picture of what is "normal" and "healthy" versus "abnormal" and "unhealthy."

For example, most kids know that it is wrong to cheat on a test. But making a decision such as whether to make out with a boy might not be as straightforward. So, relying on your own instincts and on what feels right for you becomes very important. But even a girl who stays absolutely true to herself may find herself in a difficult position, such as having a crush on another girl or her best friend's brother. It is important for girls to develop their own set of rules, while still allowing themselves the space to explore sexuality in safe and responsible ways.

Even if you feel like a total freak, it is more likely than not that you are experiencing very common and normal emotions. Remember, don't beat yourself up for thinking or even doing something freaky or weird—learn from your choices and pay close attention to your own reactions. The idea is to write your own rule-book that will help you develop at the pace that feels right for you.

XOXO,
Ashley

Pay It Forward

Remember, a healthful life is about balance. Now that you know how to walk that path, pay it forward to a friend or even to yourself! Remember the Get Healthy tips throughout this book, and then take these steps to get healthy and get going.

- Write down a timeline of when you think it is the right time/age to have your first phone call with someone you like, go on your first date, have your first kiss, etc. Ask your friends and parents for advice to make a final version. Use this is as a guideline for when to engage in certain activities.

- If you are crushing on someone who doesn't seem to share the same feelings for you, think of things you like about your crush. Think of ways to develop those qualities in yourself.

- Put together group events, such as an after-school car wash for charity, where boys and girls get a chance to get to know each other in a low-pressure, fun environment.

- Ask a parent to share one personal experience with dating or sexuality from when they were your age. See what you can learn from his or her story.

- Keep a diary of "firsts." It can be anything from "first time I babysat my little brother by myself" to "first time holding hands with a boy." This is a great private way to think about all the new experiences you are suddenly encountering.

- Visit an established health resource Web site (visit www.abdopublishing.com for safe and healthy links) to answer sex or dating questions that you are too embarrassed to ask anyone else. You may be surprised at how normal your questions actually are.

- Ask your mom or dad to take you to a clinic for pregnant teens or teens who have STDs to help you understand the real-life consequences of having unsafe, unprotected, or too-young sex.

- Research a controversial issue related to sex or dating for a school project. Examine all the different sides of the issue and invite questions and debate from your classmates.

- Go through a magazine and tear out pictures of outfits you think you would be comfortable wearing and others you think would feel overly sexy. Use this as a measure of what to wear instead of just going by what is trendy.

Additional Resources

Selected Bibliography

The Boston Women's Health Book Collective. *Our Bodies, Ourselves: A New Edition for a New Era.* New York: Simon and Schuster, 2005.

Morris Shaffer, Susan, and Linda Perlman Gordon. *Why Girls Talk—and What They're Really Saying.* New York: McGraw-Hill, 2005.

Pipher, Mary. *Reviving Ophelia: Saving the Selves of Adolescent Girls.* New York: Putnam, 1994.

Pomerantz, Shauna. *Girls, Style, and School Identities: Dressing the Part.* New York: Palgrave Macmillan, 2008.

Further Reading

Corinna, Heather. *S.E.X.: The All-You-Need-To-Know Progressive Sexuality Guide to Get You Through High School and College.* New York: Marlowe, 2007.

Harris, Robie. *It's Perfectly Normal: Changing Bodies, Growing Up, Sex, and Sexual Health.* Cambridge, MA: Candlewick Press, 2004.

Hatchell, Deborah. *What Smart Teenagers Know . . . About Dating, Relationships & Sex.* Ventura, CA: Piper Books, 2003.

Holyoke, Nancy. *A Smart Girl's Guide to Boys: Surviving Crushes, Staying True to Yourself & Other Stuff.* Middleton, WI: American Girl Publishing Inc, 2001.

Movsessian, Shushann. *Puberty Girl.* Crows Nest, N.S.W. (Australia): Allen & Unwin, 2005.

Web Sites

To learn more about relationships and sexuality, visit ABDO Publishing Company online at **www.abdopublishing.com**. Web sites about relationships and sexuality are featured on our Book Links page. These links are routinely monitored and updated to provide the most current information available.

For More Information:

For more information on this subject, contact or visit the following organizations.

Advocates for Youth

2000 M Street NW, Suite 750, Washington, DC 20036
202-419-3420
www.advocatesforyouth.org
This organization provides information to help teenagers make responsible decisions about their reproductive and sexual health.

The National Campaign to Prevent Teen and Unplanned Pregnancy

1776 Massachusetts Avenue, NW, Suite 200
Washington, DC 20036
202-478-8500
www.thenationalcampaign.org; www.stayteen.org
This group publishes information for teenagers about pregnancy, sex, love, and relationships.

Glossary

abstinence
Choosing not to have sex.

bisexual
A person who is sexually attracted to both men and women.

homosexual
A person who is sexually attracted to members of the same sex.

intimate
To be very close, often in a sexual way.

lesbian
A woman who is sexually attracted to other women.

misconception
A false or mistaken view, idea, or belief.

molest
To force sexual contact on someone.

pornography
Videos, photographs, or text that feature graphic sex.

reputation
The generally held opinion about a person or thing.

sexually active

Involvement with another person or other people in any sexual way, including sexual intercourse, touching, or other activity.

sexually transmitted disease (STD)

Any of various diseases, including chlamydia, gonorrhea, syphilis, genital herpes, and HIV, that are usually contracted through sexual intercourse or other intimate sexual contact. Also known as sexually transmitted infections (STI).

straight

A person who is sexually attracted to people of the opposite sex.

virgin

A person who has never had sex with another person.

Index

About the Author

Ashley Harris lives and works in Chicago, Illinois, where she completed an MA from the University of Chicago. Her research focused on how Web culture has impacted adolescent girls' body image and sense of identity. Her work has appeared in *VenusZine* and *Time Out Chicago*. She enjoys live music, bike riding, and spending time with the many friends whose experiences helped her write this book.

Photo Credits

Fotolia, 13, 19, 24, 31, 60; Shutterstock Images, 15, 95; Yuri Arcurs/Shutterstock Images, 27; Galina Barskaya/Shutterstock Images, 37; iStockphoto, 41; Vladimir Wrangel/Shutterstock Images, 47; Mandy Godbehear/123rf, 48; 123rf, 53; Chris Scredon/iStockphoto, 58; Galina Barskaya/Fotolia, 60; Noel Powell/Shutterstock Images, 63; Ivanna Budakova/Fotolia, 69; Mandy Godbehear/Shutterstock Images, 73; Yuri Arcurs/Fotolia, 75; Mikhail Lavrenov/Shutterstock Images, 80; Alexander Gitlits/Shutterstock Images, 84; Raisa Kanareva/Fotolia, 86; David Mzareulyan/Fotolia, 89; Monkey Business Images/Shutterstock Images, 96; Michael Jung/Shutterstock Images, 99